PETER THOMSON'S CLASSIC GOLF HOLES OF AUSTRALIA

PETER THOMSON'S CLASSIC GOLF HOLES OF AUSTRALIA

PHOTOGRAPHED BY ROGER GOULD

LOTHIAN PUBLISHING COMPANY
MELBOURNE SYDNEY AUCKLAND
PRODUCED BY ROSS PUBLISHING

THE PUBLISHER GRATEFULLY ACKNOWLEDGES
THE ASSISTANCE AND ENTHUSIASTIC SUPPORT
FOR THIS PROJECT BY MICHAEL WOLVERIDGE

First published 1988
Produced by Ross Publishing
for Lothian Publishing Company

Thomson, Peter, 1929-
  Peter Thomson's classic golf holes of Australia.

  ISBN 0 85091 336 5.

  1. Golf courses — Australia.   I. Gould, Roger.   II.
  Title.   III. Title: Classic golf holes of Australia.

796.352'06'894

Designed by Rob Cowpe Creative.
Typeset by Meredith Typesetting.
Printed by Impact Printing, Melbourne.
Production Control: Island Graphics, Melbourne.

INTRODUCTION

Everyone has their likes and dislikes, favourites and hates. In regard to golf holes and courses, I have mine. They come from a lifetime of playing the game worldwide, but particularly they come from my early experience of playing the course of my home city. In this I was very fortunate. Melbourne courses owe much to the influence of Dr Alistair Mackenzie — a giant in the field of course architecture. He visited Australia twice in the 1920s and left an indelible stamp on every course he touched. His masterpiece in Australia is the West course of the Royal Melbourne Golf Club, which even today is almost 100% Mackenzie.

But it wasn't only Royal Melbourne that benefitted from his knowledge. Almost every course or hole constructed since his departure, nearly 60 years ago, has some Mackenzie in it.

In my formative years my eye became accustomed to the Mackenzie look. I came to recognise the merit of his design. I became a believer in his philosophy of the game, as it applies to the golf holes.

He intended holes to be "enjoyable", "tempting", free from irritations and torment, and certainly free from the "humbug of lost balls". This was not just the Scotsman in him coming through. It makes the soundest common sense — just as much today as it did half a century ago.

There is a real art in golf architecture. It involves many skills and gifts. It is a tradesman's job that produces a course that makes Greg Norman's knees shake. Almost anyone can do that. It is another matter to design a course that is all things to all manner of golfers. Royal Melbourne West, and East for that matter, is such a course.

Mackenzie was a great lover of the Old Course at St Andrews. He did not design it. Nature did. But he fathomed the real truth of its worth, and he used features of that famous links in many places. I, too, love the Old Course. I did so from first sight, perhaps because of growing up on Melbourne courses. Having seen as it were, a lot of copies I suddenly came across the original!

I have no apology to offer for my prejudice, and I do not ask everyone to agree with me. Nor do I suggest this anthology includes *all* the best holes in Australia. These are just the ones I know of and appreciate.

They are beautifully depicted by Roger Gould to whom I am grateful. I am grateful also to John Ross for putting it all together and accepting my pronouncements in good faith.

The vista of golf is infinitely variable, but there is an essence of balance and proportion in the best holes. I hope we have captured it.

ROYAL MELBOURNE GOLF CLUB, MELBOURNE

Fourth Hole, West Course. Par Five. 430 Metres.

Royal Melbourne can claim with justification to have Australia's best course. Both East and West layouts are outstanding in their contour and design, however the combination of the two, known as the 'Composite' is better than either. The Composite comprises 12 holes of the West course and six of the East, all contained within the home paddock. It is for this reason used for big events.

The most stunning of these holes is the 14th (or the West's 4th). In length it hovers between par four and five but as either serves its purpose. It comprises in the first place an awesome tee shot over gaping bunkers cut deep into the crest of the highest point of the course. Against a strong wind only a small percentage of players can carry across. The next must use the longer route to the left. From the ideal spot the second shot is a particularly testing one for the fact it must be played from a downhill lie, to skirt some natural areas of wilderness including the native flora and two large, deep, steep walled bunkers. It is reachable by the mighty and the challenge is there, irresistible. The penalty for transgression can be serious, but the reward is thrilling. Coming where it does in the round this hole often decides the results of championships. Dare I say it is Australia's best hole?

ROYAL MELBOURNE GOLF CLUB, MELBOURNE

Fifth Hole, West Course. Par Three. 161 Metres

One-shot holes across valleys abound in courses all over the world. They have no prototype in classic links golf since the game's original courses were flat. But somewhere along the line the urge to hit 'all-carry' shots to a perfectly visible target became a must in course architecture. The Composite 5th (also West 5th) is a superb example of this type of hole. The view from the tee is inspiring, but even for the best of players the scoring possibilities lie between one and six. The green, of admirable proportion and shape, has a decided tilt from back to front and given the usual glassy speed of all Royal Melbourne greens, putting from far off can be very testing indeed, particularly downhill. Three and even four putts are common for the careless or over exuberent. To miss the target with the tee shot is to compound the woes. Altogether an outstanding piece of architecture.

ROYAL MELBOURNE GOLF CLUB, MELBOURNE

Sixth Hole, West Course. Par Four. 391 Metres

As long par fours go the 6th comprises the best of all features pertaining to classic architecture. It has a tee shot encouraging all out hitting with a gamble, a second shot demanding proficiency and a green of deceptive contour. Of 391 m it is a dog-leg right, with a difference, in that no trees intrude. Too many dog-leg holes hinge around tall trees which allow for no options and therefore no temptations, adding up to second rate architecture. Here at the 6th, depending on the wind you bite off all you can chew. One can cut considerable length from this hole by driving across the bracken and rushes. Taking the safe but long way around converts this hole to par five length. Therein lies its charm. It's bite comes with the putting. Some deft touch is required downhill, while crosshill putts call for some imagination and judgement.

ROYAL MELBOURNE GOLF CLUB, MELBOURNE

Seventh Hole, West Course. Par Three. 135 Metres

This intriguing little hole is an afterthought. Dr Mackenzie's original hole lay in the way of the first hole of a new East Course, consequently the hole was moved to its present location. As it stands it is a fine hole, the like of which I have not seen anywhere. Not many uphill par threes come off, but this one does. Set on the skyline, its putting surface is largely obscured except for the small section that reveals itself on the left front. The green is surrounded on three sides by sand, the front bunker being particularly deep and straight faced — such as one can find at St Andrews. This must be avoided at all costs, yet to over-shoot is also heavily penalised, for the green slopes violently from back to front and escape from beyond is seldom unpunished. The foreground is left covered by indigenous plants adding importantly to the general aesthetics. It is a proud little hole of high merit.

ROYAL MELBOURNE GOLF CLUB, MELBOURNE

Sixteenth Hole, East Course. Par Three. 153 Metres

An unusual little hole that might happily fit into the Composite course if 19 holes were allowed. The pattern of bunkering is unique creating a large choice of cup settings all of which prompt pinpoint accuracy. The hole takes the form of a gentle 'drop-shot' from a tee ground higher than the green, allowing for the green to be more or less flat. No terror of any kind is present, but this is a pleasurable hole, inviting confidence.

ROYAL MELBOURNE GOLF CLUB, MELBOURNE

Eighteenth Hole, East Course. Eighteenth Hole, Composite Course. Par Four. 395 Metres

As a finishing hole of big championships the 18th of Royal Melbourne (Composite and East) ranks with the world's best. It is a par four of powerful length set into the prevailing wind. On a grand scale its size and proportion belie its difficulty. A score of four is a meritorious accomplishment in any circumstance, but especially so in winning a big event. At this hole there is no substitute for powerful swinging and precise hitting — just the examination you would demand of a tournament winner. The hole is unique in having no fairway bunkering, indeed there is a 'football field' to drive at. It is often in these circumstances of freedom that a player will throw all caution to the wind and unhappily hook a tee shot into the only place to avoid — a copse of dense tea-tree on the left side. From wherever the second shot is played, it must be accurately directed to whichever quarter of the green is hosting the flag, for the contours of this immense green work against long putts. The bunkering is spectacular, and the island of wilderness therein extraordinary.

ROYAL ADELAIDE GOLF CLUB, ADELAIDE

Third Hole. Par Four. 275 Metres

A former Captain of the Royal Adelaide once told me he judged Royal Adelaide the best course he'd seen in Australia. In pure golfing terms it could very well be. "Seaton", as it is affectionately known, is by no means a beauty propped up against say, Augusta National, but beauty is in the eye of the beholder, isn't it? One only has to play Royal Adelaide to appreciate its class. It is almost a golf links, in that links are flat. But the sea has long since receded from Seaton so that its territory is a patchwork of sand and soil. Recently modernised, it retains its true character and the 3rd hole, one of the more famous, is untouched. It comprises a tee shot through a narrow trough between a sand ridge on one side and a thick copse of pines on the other. In its best condition ice plant covers the sand in the way it does at famous Cypress Point in California. The green is an unexceptional piece of putting. Running the gauntlet of troubles along the way makes this hole a gem. May it ever be so!

ROYAL ADELAIDE GOLF CLUB, ADELAIDE

Sixth Hole. Par Four. 395 Metres

With a prevailing wind blowing from the South West this 6th hole is top class. Natural looking mounds define the fairway until a cross ridge intervenes but the key shot is the approach. Most days a long iron is needed to make the distance to a tilted green looking squarely at the striker. Nature's troubles abound so that it is not easy to get away with dribbles, but then it would seem to be impossible to get yourself "out-of-play". This is a thoroughly enjoyable challenging par four — one of the best of many on this course.

ROYAL ADELAIDE GOLF CLUB

Seventh Hole. Par Three. 143 Metres

A first class par three this one, and beautifully bunkered with seven small pot type traps. They give this hole a special look — one that for me suggests it belongs in Scotland, where such things are common and natural. Consider the alternative — one or two large broad bunkers. It would not look as good as it does, would it? It would not have that stamp of class. Like the previous hole this one is laid out heading south west into the prevailing wind. The wind then is a vital feature of this hole, calling for skilled stroke making. Without wind it has few teeth, but then that goes for almost any hole. This is one of Australia's best looking par threes — one I would like to play on any course.

ROYAL ADELAIDE GOLF CLUB

Fourteenth Hole. Par Four. 404 Metres

There are several places on Royal Adelaide's fine course that remind one of seaside Britain. One is an area of wilderness that must be skirted (or carried) from the 14th tee. There is no finer piece of classic architecture anywhere on our continent that I know. Such things are precious and should be on a National Golf Heritage Register so that some future vandal does not get the notion to 'tidy it up'. The tee ground abutting the Seaton Railway track is a piece of Australiana. This might be quaint to some, but to me it is the character of Royal Adelaide. I must mention the green, which is set on a sand ridge amid a thin copse of pines. I like every aspect of this unusual hole. It is high class.

ROYAL ADELAIDE GOLF CLUB

Eighteenth Hole. Par Four. 390 Metres

The 'home rule' here at Royal Adelaide might have been plucked from St Andrews or Princes, Deal. It has distinct flatness, just a hint of mounding around the green. There are bunkers below ground on the right, and a dangerous wet ditch on the left, but these are not apparent to the player of the second shot. Nothing wrong with that. Dangers out of eye are more fearsome, but there is no rule of architecture that demands that trouble should always be obvious. Or any rule that greens should make perfect targets. There is some deception here, making the second shot so much more difficult — appropriate to a final hole where everything is at stake — even a two dollar wager!

KINGSTON HEATH GOLF CLUB, MELBOURNE

Third Hole. Par Four. 271 Metres

Here is a first class drive and pitch hole, made outstanding by a well conceived green and some interesting subterranean traps as well. The pitch shot may be the shortest shot in golf, but it is by no means the easiest. Lofting a 50 metre shot to a table top green requires a perfect judgement and execution. Even some top class players never quite master this stroke, even though they be infallible drivers. All good reason then to include such holes in the best of layouts, provided the features are right, like a gentle dogleg, an unplayable place or two for the tiger who attempts to devour such a hole with sheer power, and a green that accepts and holds only the shot well struck with the grooves of the club face. This hole has it all and is at the same time an enjoyable hole of nice dimension.

KINGSTON HEATH GOLF CLUB

Fifteenth Hole. Par Three. 142 Metres

The chance to use a hill of pure white sand for some kind of short hole was more than Kingston Heath's original planners could let pass. Of such terrain is what golf architects' dreams are made. The end result of their inspiration is one of Australia's best short holes. Of just 142 m, uphill, the hole asks for bullseye accuracy. The consequences of missing the target can be very expensive. The bunkers are extensive and cavernous. One can imagine the terror they must have struck in the early days before the invention of the round soled sand iron. Trying to escape from these with a sharp edged niblick must have led to many a torn up card! Even with modern implements the shots demanded from the bunkers are of the highest skill, especially if the sand is soft. Not too many attempters 'get down in two'. The green itself is small in size and is tilted steeply from back to front. This feature is enough to cause the trembles. The 15th is not a hole for the faint-hearted. In concept it is brilliant.

KOOYONGA GOLF CLUB, ADELAIDE

First Hole. Par Five. 500 Metres

Kooyonga is one of my favourite courses. It is a concise layout on beautiful sand, incorporating some absolutely outstanding holes. Not many famous courses start with a par five, but there is nothing wrong with that. When it comes down to the bottom line, a par five consists of two drives and a pitch, as against a short par four which is one drive and a pitch. At this hole the green is set above the fairway in a saddle of the sand ridge — an appropriate enough place for it, as it virtually precludes the chance of 'getting home in two'. Even so everything is possible especially as balls become aerodynamically better and shafts improve their energy output. This hole however should stand the test of time, and stand as tall in the year 2001 as it does today.

KOOYONGA GOLF CLUB, ADELAIDE

Second Hole. Par Four. 437 Metres

This is a superb par four in a classic setting of natural sand ridges. Usually played into a head wind it makes a formidable par four, not so easily accomplished by anyone. The fairway is made of the low ground between the ridges. The green sits a little higher above the water table, making an interesting target. This is perhaps the best par four of many fine ones at Kooyonga and a joy to behold!

KOOYONGA GOLF CLUB, ADELAIDE

Tenth Hole. Par Four. 407 Metres

Kooyonga course has multipersonality according to the change of terrain. This adds to its charm. The whole of the second nine seems a different character to the first. However, each hole stands on its own merit and the tenth hole is one of the best. It runs along the east side of the wetland of the course headed south into the wind, making a strong par of four that might be beyond most players. This type and length of hole is very enticing to me. I enjoy thinking of that second shot as a low raking two iron into a stiff, cool breeze. Such are daydreams made of.

KOOYONGA GOLF CLUB, ADELAIDE

Seventeenth Hole. Par Four. 342 Metres

This is a highly unusual hole, joining a list of particularly exciting penultimate holes around the nation. There is first a drive to (or over) a high ridge with a yawning bunker starting from the left. This shot is perhaps enough aggravation for any hole, but that is only half of it. The second shot must be played with a medium to short iron, across a sizeable pond which laps against the right front of the green. There is, as there always should be on any planned hole, an escape route around the left side, for those of us less sure of ourselves. For the super player though there is the excitement of the shot to the back right hand corner — the real championship spot on the green. This then is a fine hole of maximum flexibility, making an exciting adventure for all standards of golfers.

PENINSULA GOLF CLUB, FRANKSTON, VICTORIA

Seventeenth Hole, South Course. Par Four. 393 Metres

Peninsula was changed and relocated many years ago, but it was possible to keep some of the old design. The finest of these relics has become the 17th on the South Course. It is a very strong hole, coming at an important part of the finishing run. A good par four allows strokes to be interchanged, depending on one's mood or talent. A drive and seven iron for one player may be a three wood and four iron for another. Such possibilities give a hole character, and the 17th abounds in these ingredients. Framed by natural woodland the hole is bunkered in front of the tee, inviting the tee shot to be aimed left. This is a clever arrangement because those who avoid the danger by too much are then confronted by a virtually impossible second shot across a yawning bunker which guards the left side of the green. Once reached the green is appropriately straight forward.

SORRENTO GOLF CLUB, SORRENTO, VICTORIA

First Hole. Par Four. 295 Metres

Sorrento Golf Club has one of the best courses beyond the Melbourne metropolitan areas. Sited near the heads of Port Phillip Bay it occupies some undulating land of sand and limestone. It offers a great variety of holes, all of unusual interest and is generally in top condition. Rebuilt and lengthened in the 1970s, it changed from a summer holiday course to full size — one now capable of holding any level of event. The first hole is an inviting shot from a tee high on the club house hill, across a valley to a ridge of fine turf with an impressive expanse of sand on the lower right side to worry about. Sorrento is seldom without wind from some direction, which gives this shot its basic fun. From the ridge it is a short pitch to a subtle green — narrow but deep with a sharp fall off on the left side. This hole is always inspiring. Even to stand on the tee and "play" an imaginary drive is something any golfer will enjoy. What a picture!

VICTORIA GOLF CLUB, MELBOURNE

Fourth Hole. Par Three. 170 Metres

The best par threes are usually the result of clever siting on the part of the designer. Such astuteness is apparent in the 4th hole. Of 175 m fully stretched, it makes a challenging target — all of the green being highly visible, rising gently from front to back and falling off steeply into the natural slopes accentuated into classical deep bunkering disappearing below view. In its original construction the green "sat there" in a sea of white sand, which must have been an awe-inspiring sight, but after nearly 60 years intruding grasses have covered all but the below ground hazards. The hole provides a stern test of stroke-making, no matter which way the wind blows. It is one of Victoria's many strong holes.

VICTORIA GOLF CLUB, MELBOURNE

Eighth Hole. Par Five. 475 Metres

The 8th is another fine example of artistic use of terrain. Before newly planted trees intruded on the line, the green could be seen from the tee 50 m away rising up from an extended shallow depression to make an exciting target. Even now this hole has an inviting aspect as the fairway bottle-necks at the range of the tee shot, then opens out into a generous 'Elysian Field', only to develop into a narrow passage between some daunting traps. Powerful players can occasionally reach this green in two shots, but it is cleverly tilted contrary to the fairway and is consequently difficult to 'hit'. This aspect of its design sets it apart to rank as a first class par five of sensible fairness — an encouragement to all golfers regardless of proficiency. Is not that a test of class?

VICTORIA GOLF CLUB, MELBOURNE

Seventeenth Hole. Par Five. 520 Metres

Penultimate holes the world over often have some difficulty about them that brings a course to its climax. (I think of the Road Hole on the Old Course at St Andrews.) Victoria's 17th falls into this category. For a start it is the longest hole on the course at 520 m. It has seldom been reached in two shots, which is hardly surprising taking into account its undulation and its shape as a long right curling fairway. The shots pitch onto an upslope (again inferring clever layout planning), entertaining three threatening bunkers on the high side. This has the effect of forcing play to the lower right side which demands that the second shot of anything like full length has to be 'bent' in a slice manner. Trouble awaits the mis-directed on both sides, but the special feature of this hole comes at the putting end. The green slopes steeply from back to low front. At championship time when greens are all cut close and in mid-winter when growth is sparse, putting downhill can be scary. This means usually a pitch to a below the hole position is essential to any hopes of a birdie four. This is an especially adventurous hole, full of character.

ROYAL SYDNEY GOLF CLUB, SYDNEY

First Hole. Par Four. 256 Metres

I give full marks to opening holes of drive and pitch length. There are many on Australian golf courses, and this one at Royal Sydney is better than most. The hole has a variable set of tees. The championship tee is high up near clubhouse level. From such height all is laid out ahead — bunkers, rough, trees and the green, all in plain view. The bunkers are of sufficient depth and scale to be feared, which is important on such a short par four. The green is a rambling shape and not altogether receptive, especially on its right-hand end. It all adds up to a very worthy opener to one of our top courses.

ROYAL SYDNEY GOLF CLUB, SYDNEY

Second Hole. Par Five. 500 Metres

This is a new hole of 1986 vintage — the old hole extended at both ends to make a round par five. The silver expanses of sand along the right hand length are preserved in full view, giving the hole its classic look. With the wind against, this hole is a fearsome par five. Played down wind it is an equally testing hole when the hope is a birdie four. The green is of a size appropriate for a hole of this length. A deep straight-faced bunker stands sentinel at the entrance, backed up by a squadron standing by to the right. This is a hole full of possibilities in the matter of scores, but I consider a birdie four well earned, and a par not to be despised.

ROYAL SYDNEY GOLF CLUB, SYDNEY

Eighth Hole. Par Four. 276 Metres

Here is a hole of unusual length, 276 m, on occasions of helpful wind, driveable. Yet the scale of everything makes the par of four a satisfactory accomplishment to even the mighty. Appropriately, the hole has a narrow fairway tapering to a bottleneck before the green. The green contorts from a low draining apron to a high table top at the right rear. The surrounds are steeply falling away, so that any shot less than precisely struck will inevitably find discomfort. Every course should have a hole of this type. It is a nice examination of pitching skill with just a hint of outrage!

ROYAL SYDNEY GOLF CLUB, SYDNEY

Eighteenth Hole, Par Four. 375 Metres.

Top courses usually finish with a flourish and this is no exception. With the clubhouse for background this makes a magnificent setting for a tense finish before a large crowd of spectators, or just a foursome in the bar. The hole doglegs left around a swampy wood, the second shot asking for pinpoint accuracy to ensure par. A famous setting.

PORT DOUGLAS MIRAGE

Second Hole. Par Three. 160 Metres

This is a very attractive par three of 160 m. In a superb natural tropical setting it is one of the prettiest holes I have seen. Nor is it just a pretty face. It is a well bunkered green of two levels and just enough dimension to receive a well hit shot and reject a mishit. Australia is in a new era of course development in tropical climes. Modern hybrid grasses can make stunning fairways and greens and if nature can be seduced to come along, the whole result can be glorious. The time will come when courses in the tropics are ranked with those in traditional temperate places. It is holes like this one that will pull the game in that direction.

PORT DOUGLAS MIRAGE

Seventeenth Hole. Par Four. 400 Metres

Penultimate holes in the wide world of golf are often the crisis point of a round. This may all stem from the Road Hole at St Andrews, which is arguably the prototype. It makes good sense to lead a golfer through an adventure story of unexpected twists and turns, then put him through the wringer at the 17th. The last hole can then be a happy epilogue. That's the scenario anyway, and who can put it to the sword? It is as good as any. Here at Port Douglas the 17th hole is by far the most dangerous, difficult, character testing of the course. The hole skirts the mangrove on the left side — all the way to the green. Two bunkers announce the dangers. Off to the right is first the 'Himalayan Mounds', some short strip of rough and at the 220 m distance, the inland lake. All this adds up to a very testing tee shot, which because of the hole's length, needs to be a long one. The second shot aims at a large green, half of which tucks behind a substantial bunker. Not the eternal fascination of the Road Hole, but a worthy example. A thrilling hole.

YARRA YARRA GOLF CLUB, MELBOURNE

Fifth Hole. Par Four. 400 Metres

I don't condemn blind shots the way many do. I recognise them to be difficult but not unreasonable, especially if there are some guides to help you get your bearings. The tee shot on the 5th hole is driven over a crest into a large-size (by modern standards) reception area. Huge eucalypts indicate the limits to the right hand side and there are other sighters in the far off distance. Once over this hurdle, the sailing is plain — a long iron perhaps uphill to a deep green bunkered both sides. I have a fondness for this hole. I think it inspires the best in us!

YARRA YARRA GOLF CLUB, MELBOURNE

Ninth Hole. Par Five. 473 Metres

The Yarra Yarra course was designed by Alex Russell, by then a partner of Alistair Mackenzie. It is of no wonder that he imposed many of the features and techniques he learnt at Royal Melbourne. This 9th is very much a Royal Melbourne hole, using large scale bunkering such as can be found at Black Rock, and a green of profound undulation — the equal of anything the Grand Master has ever done himself! Par five crosses a valley in accepted fashion, dog-legging around meandering sand and rising up in its second half to a high green. This hole is often reached in two shots, but that in no way disqualifies it. On the contrary, its length is a sporting challenge to pull it off, nothing but the finest shots succeeding. Even so reaching the green does not guarantee any birdie. There is considerable challenge in two putting, and it could be a fact this 9th has seen more three putts than any green in Melbourne! When I think of Yarra Yarra, I think of this 9th hole.

YARRA YARRA GOLF CLUB, MELBOURNE

Eleventh Hole. Par Three. 165 Metres

Alex Russell must have been inspired to create this par three. It not only looks good — it is good! Yet on its opening day it must have caused something of a sensation. By modern standards it is very difficult as par threes go. Back in 1930 it must have been a stunner. It is to the club's great credit that nothing has been done over the years to modify it by, say, filling in the bunker high to the left. The green is narrow. It lies askew to the line of play and rises through three levels. It is unique as far as I know. Even in this far end of the 20th Century, I would doubt if I could see its like elsewhere.

ALICE SPRINGS GOLF CLUB, NORTHERN TERRITORY

Third Hole. Par Three. 167 Metres

The healthiest golf on earth is desert golf. Older people's bones do not ache with dampness, and the dry air has the added advantage that it allows the ball to fly further. It is no wonder that Palm Springs, U.S.A. believes it is the 'Golf Capital of the World'. Australia's one contribution to this form of golf is in the Red Centre at the Alice Springs Golf Club, where the desert has been transformed into an oasis. Restricted water has demanded a layout of island tees, island fairways and island greens. The hazard is the desert stretching for 1000 miles all around. The par three third is set beneath the spectacular McDonnell Range. The tee is set high on a rocky peninsula, requiring a shot across 100 metres of desert to the pulpit green, guarded in front by a large crater bunker. The need for accuracy and length make it a difficult proposition. The course is at its scenic best when the wildflowers are blooming in the spring, or when the sun is setting along the range.

ALICE SPRINGS GOLF CLUB, NORTHERN TERRITORY

Eighth Hole. Par Four. 391 Metres

Nature has a big hand in creating a valley hole, such as the eighth at Alice Springs. It is flanked on either side by rocky desert ridges, leaving room for a generous landing area about 60 metres wide. Play is slightly downhill from the tee and a formal bunker is set at driving distance on the right hand side. The green is tightly guarded by a nest of bunkers short and to the right. Large lemon scented gums short and left of the big green, create the complete desert picture.

ROYAL CANBERRA GOLF CLUB, CANBERRA

Fourteenth Hole. Par Four. 415 Metres

This is a solid par four with exceptional good looks and just a peep view of Lake Burley Griffin off to the right. From a raised tee the drive lands on a slight upslope — always useful design to effectively lengthen a hole — large, open flat bunkers fill the left side to set off the target. From there a long iron to a large green of two levels with a small step. This is not a punishing frightening hole, just an honest to goodness long par four — one full of merit with everything in place.

ROYAL CANBERRA GOLF CLUB, CANBERRA

Eighteenth Hole. Par Five. 520 Metres

This is a magnificent final hole of effectively 550 m since the second half of it climbs uphill. Thick forest lines both sides — inhibiting all-out thumping — creating a stunning natural arena for high drama. This green is huge — nearly 800 square metres — made of three convoluting levels and a minimum of sand to worry about. It is a man size hole in all respects — with every par scored a capital effort. One of Australia's best holes.

COMMONWEALTH GOLF CLUB, MELBOURNE

Sixteenth Hole. Par Four. 359 Metres.

Commonwealth Golf Club has the best shaped bunkers in Australia. Built in reverse curve (i.e. below ground) they present a spectacular aspect particularly when the sun is low. This fine course is built around its bunkers, greens being of generally smaller size than other championship venues. This is a very acceptable feature, something that lifts the course well above the ordinary. Water holes are rare in Melbourne. Or at any rate they were at the time of Commonwealth's beginnings. The thought of a ball lost so near the line of play was anathema to people who considered a golf ball an expensive item! However Commonwealth had its lake, or swamp to better define it. There seemed no harm in playing alongside it, even skirting around it. As it has turned out the 16th hole has endured and become even popular. Perhaps it was ahead of its kind, but it must have been a fearsome hole in hickory times. Even today it presents a problem. A warning sign — don't drive left — and then don't be chicken either, because from the extreme right side of the fairway, the green side bunker comes into play and the green itself slopes away left, presenting a small target. This is a clever hole and a pretty picture. It has the capacity to separate men from boys. From my early days I remember the tale of the local player who lost three balls in the lake and threw his clubs in after them!

METROPOLITAN GOLF CLUB

First Hole. Par Four. 380 Metres

The Metropolitan Club is justifiably proud of its trees, especially about the old original part of the course which largely comprises the first nine holes. Magnificent eucalypts and malaleucas line each fairway, setting each hole in a decorative frame. The opening hole is typical. Lined along both sides the fairway bends gently left at the 200 m mark to present a picture of golf architecture at its best. This part of the course is built on sand. The bunkers were constructed by horse and drag-scoop, digging deep into the flat terrain. Well placed too, allowing an open approach apron stepping up to a slightly raised green. This is by no means a weak hole allowing some latitude. No 1 could fit in anywhere along the sequence of holes, and even make a fine finishing hole. But as a first hole it sets the character of the course, prepares one for things to come!

METROPOLITAN GOLF CLUB, MELBOURNE

Second Hole. Par Three. 144 Metres

What a charming little hole is this one! A rare breed in fact. So natural and tempting — a green set in what appears to be a sea of bracken and rushes! Yet there is happy deception here. The target is bigger than it might appear and at 144 m it is easily hit with a high lofted shot. Par threes of this length are rarely constructed in these modern times. More is the pity. Golf holes should not all be irksome and unforgiving. This hole is for fun and joy with just a hint of whimsy.

METROPOLITAN GOLF CLUB, MELBOURNE

Third Hole. Par Four. 395 Metres

I enthuse about holes that have some sort of natural short rough in front of the tee. To me this feature imprints some nature into the scene, lifting my spirits. The old holes at Metropolitan use this device to perfection and the 3rd hole is a good example. The view from the tee out through the chute to close mown fairway is superb and inviting. However, the hole doesn't end there. This smart par four has a stepped green high at the rear and a cavernous bunker guarding the left side. Into the prevailing wind this shot is very demanding and therefore rewarding to pull off. I give this hole full-marks for naturalness and character.

METROPOLITAN GOLF CLUB, MELBOURNE

Fifth Hole. Par Four. 355 Metres

Par fours come in all shapes and sizes. This one is unlike any other I know about. First a drive up a slight slope with not that wide a fairway to hit. Driving uphill is never straightforward and a legitimate device for designers. This one is fair enough. From the crest of the fairway the second shot is a small descent to a green sloping steeply to the left. Greenside bunkers on the right and the left, and in front that fast disappearing space on our courses — a chipping area. I wonder if this hole would look striking without the backdrop of the massive aged eucalypts, but there they are in all their glory, giving this hole a distinctive image.

METROPOLITAN GOLF CLUB, MELBOURNE

Eighth Hole. Par Five. 476 Metres

This is one of Metropolitan's old and original masterpieces that has stood the test of time. It is no ordinary par five that can be reached in two with nothing but power. Here the examination of shot-making is stern and punishment for anything wayward is severe — perhaps too much so, because unplayables and even lost balls are a possibility along both sides of its 476 m. Even so I put it down amongst the best holes I know. It is narrow in the modern sense, bunkered with a good plan, and ends with a green cleverly contrived. I have seen threes and eights scored here on the same day which is to perhaps endorse its attributes, but overall it is a beautiful hole with plenty to admire.

NEW SOUTH WALES GOLF CLUB, SYDNEY

Sixth Hole. Par Three. 181 Metres

Who would leave out a hole such as this? Generally, the laws of our country don't allow us to use our land edges for golf holes. Pity. Such holes in other places are famous. This is the only one we've got in our metropolitan areas, so it is something special. Not just to look at either. This can be a tricky hole to play. Especially in a cross wind. The proportions are just right, making a superb and beautiful hole.

BARWON HEADS GOLF CLUB, VICTORIA

Thirteenth Hole. Par Three. 133 Metres

Barwon Heads is the only golf course in Australia set on the sort of links lands — the rough, sandy margins between the sea and solid ground — that inspired the original game of golf. It is a test of all things, including man against the elements. The moisture laden wind, when it is blowing, is different to an inland wind, and one must judge the weight of the wind in shotmaking. At the 13th the tee looks down on a pulpit green which sits alone in a wild sea of sand dunes and scrub. It is a remarkable test of character and improvisation.

BARWON HEADS GOLF CLUB, VICTORIA

Third Hole. Par Four. 380 Metres

As golf developed quarries and craters were the next most obvious place, after links land, to create golf courses. Many courses around London were created on the heathland which grew over disused gravel quarries. Barwon Heads yet again deserves special mention on offering this superb quarry hole. The design invites us to drive as close as we can to the long chasm. It is important on this strong par four to get a good tee shot away to set up for the long second to the plateau green.

HUNTINGDALE GOLF CLUB, MELBOURNE

Third Hole. Par three. 149 Metres

Huntingdale course is characterised by large, mainly flat greens, but this 3rd hole is an exception in having a green of two levels of about a metre difference. There are then two separate targets and woe betide the player who plays to the wrong level. There is nothing subtle about this hole. Everything is perfectly obvious, but it does cause trembles. Top players are wont to stumble here, especially in a good wind. It can be conquered with a smartly hit short iron — to the appropriate level of course; but should never be taken lightly.

ROGER GOULD WISHES TO THANK
PETER RATTRAY OF KODAK (AUSTRALASIA PTY. LTD.)
AND
HEINZ HUBER OF WILD LEITZ (AUSTRALIA) PTY. LTD.
FOR THEIR HELP IN THE PRODUCTION OF THIS BOOK

KODAK FILM • LEICA CAMERAS